CHRISTMAS IN AMERICA

BY ANTONIA FELIX

COURAGE
BOOKS

AN IMPRINT OF RUNNING PRESS
PHILADELPHIA • LONDON

9   8   7   6   5   4   3   2   1
Digit on the right indicates the number of this printing.

Library of Congress Cataloging-in-Publication Number
99-072468

ISBN 0-7624-0594-5

This book was designed and produced by
TODTRI Book Publishers
P. O. Box 572, New York, NY 10116-0572
Fax: (212) 695-6984
e-mail: todtri@mindspring.com

Author: Antonia Felix

Publisher: Robert M. Tod
Senior Editor: Edward Douglas
Book Designer: Mark Weinberg
Typesetting: Command-O Design

Printed and bound in Singapore

Published by Courage Books,
an imprint of Running Press Book Publishers
125 South Twenty-second Street
Philadelphia, PA 19103-4399

Visit us on the web!
www.runningpress.com

PICTURE CREDITS

CONTENTS

The Origins of Christmas in America — A Brief History

"It is not strange that the Americans, as a creative people, have peculiar and varied ways of their own in keeping this, the most remarkable day in the calendar."
—FROM *CHRISTMAS: ITS ORIGIN AND ASSOCIATIONS*: LONDON, 1902

Stockings hanging on the mantlepiece, home-made Christmas dinner with all the trimmings, band concerts in the school, carolers at the mall, piles of gifts under a brightly lit Christmas tree. The American Christmas is an astonishing mixture of old and new. Each region has its own unique traditions that reflect America's rich cultural inheritance from every corner of the world, making Christmas the grandest melting pot of holidays. From the quaint New England Christmas in Massachusetts to the luminous Las Posadas processions of the Southwest to the glitzy Hollywood Christmas parade, no other holiday celebrates the glorious diversity of America like Christmas.

A few essentials of Christmas such as Santa Claus, gift-giving, and the Christmas tree are permanent fixtures from coast to coast. The heart-warming effects they bring, year after year, are timeless. But these traditions are quite young in terms of America's complete history. The Christmas that is familiar today was born in the late 1800s, and the celebration did not become a national holiday until 1890. Drawing from the traditions of the places they left behind in Europe, American immigrants brought Christmas to every corner of the new land. Each nationality left its mark it a special way, and during the holiday season American households are filled with warm, personal glimpses of history.

The Anti-Christmas Puritans

Christmas in the Puritan colonies was nothing like Thanksgiving. In fact, for many Puritans Christmas didn't exist at all. In most of colonial America, December twenty-fifth was just a day like any other. The Puritans did not observe this day as a sacred holiday because the date of Jesus' birth does not appear in the Bible. They believed that the Christmas they left behind in England was a frivolous holiday that just gave people an excuse for noisy rabble-rousing and drunkenness. The Puritan sentiment against Christmas was so strong that the holiday was outlawed in some colonies, and fines were given out to those who were caught celebrating the day by not showing up for work.

While Thanksgiving was full of meaning, a family time for celebrating the bounty of the New World, Christmas didn't stir the hearts of the Puritans. Their severe opinion of the holiday came from their experience of Christmas in the Old World. For hundreds of years, December had been a month of rowdy festivities in the agricultural societies of Europe. This was the only month in which meat was slaughtered, because the cold weather kept it from spoiling. It was also the time when beer and ales had fermented and were ready to drink. Farmers also enjoyed precious leisure time in these weeks after the harvest and before the new planting season. These circumstances, along with a deeply imbedded history of celebrating the winter solstice, made December a carnival month in countries such as Britain, France, Germany, and Holland.

Year after year, a few December rituals became very popular. These customs included wassailing, in which groups of young men would barge in to a home,

OPPOSITE: The very nature of Christmas— the celebration of the birth of a child—makes this, above all others, a day devoted to the cherishing of the young. The parts they play in Christmas ceremonies, therefore, are especially moving and poignant.

SUPPLEMENT, JANUARY 1, 1876.]   HARPER'S WEEKLY.   17

SEEING SANTA CLAUS.

HULLO! what's the matter? Who's this that I see!
Two forms on the roof! Who on earth can they be?
It is time that the young ones were tucked in their beds,
With visions of Christmas afloat in their heads.

Now bother these boys! What the mischief, I say,
Has brought them up here, just to be in my way!
But stop! a thought strikes me. Aha! now I see:
They are waiting, the scamps for a good look at me.

Oh dear, how they stare! What on earth shall I do?
Do you think, you young scamps, I'll be conquered by you?
You seem very bright, with your wide-open eyes,
And you'd think it so smart to take me by surprise.

It's a very fine plan, my young rascals, but pause
Ere you get up a trap to catch old Santa Claus.
And then, I'm afraid, if I let you succeed—

That I've nothing to do but to pack up my toys,
And call once a year on the girls and the boys;
That my reindeers are harnessed and ready to fly
Quick, quick o'er the roofs and the chimneys so high.

Ah, what would you say could you know the sad truth?
Long ago in your service I wore out my youth.
Just think of the burdens I've borne on my back,

ABOVE: *One of the creators of today's image of Santa Claus was Thomas Nast, whose illustrations forever captured the costume, style, and manner of "the jolly old elf," as chracterized in Clement C. Moore's famous poem.*

York, Philadelphia, and Boston complained about the noisy gangs of men who took over the streets at Christmas and New Year's, shooting off guns and fireworks, breaking into homes, and wreaking havoc all over the city. The carnival atmosphere of the holiday season lives on in our time. In Philadelphia, where the biggest mumming (costume) parade of the nineteenth century was held, the tradition returns every year in the no-holds-barred New Year's Day Mummers Parade.

Christmas outside New England had a more festive flavor in the eighteenth century, especially for the wealthy. In the South, plantations lavishly offered parties, dances, dinners, hunts, games, and other amusements. The Puritan influences of the northern colonies could not reach these regions. In Virginia and throughout the South, lavish balls, dinner parties, and even fox-hunts were arranged for the holidays, keeping Christmas in the style of England and France.

A Poem and a Cartoon: Beginnings of the Modern Christmas

Christmas as an at-home holiday, a festive day with a focus on children and the family, developed in the prosperous times after the Civil War. By the turn of the century, Christmas had become fully commercialized, complete with advertisements for proper gentlemen's and ladies' gifts, Christmas card companies, and, most importantly, appearances by Santa Claus in department stores.

We owe much of the look of the American Christmas to three gentlemen from New York. At the center of the story is the creation of that beloved, bearded Christmas visitor, Santa Claus. This figure was drawn from St. Nicholas, a bishop who lived in fourth-century Asia Minor, and whose feast day on December 6 had been celebrated for hundreds of years in Europe. Children celebrated St. Nicholas' feast day by hanging up stockings that would miraculously fill with small gifts overnight. The Dutch settlers in New York held to their favorite stories and verses about Sinti Nikolaas, or Sinti Klaus, whose American name would become Santa Claus.

sing songs, and demand drink and refreshment in return for a gesture of good will for the year to come. People would exchange clothing with the opposite sex and pay visits to each other in disguise. Drinking, eating, dancing, singing, and making fun of the landowners and the ruling class were all part of this December merry-making. Historians believe that it was an important way of venting the pressure that was felt between the classes throughout most of the year.

These riotous celebrations found their way to the New World, and the Puritans tried very hard to quash them. As late as the early 1800s, newspapers in New

The old Dutch version of St. Nicholas was made popular in a bestselling book by New Yorker Washington Irving. In Diedrich Knickerbocker's History of New York, Irving describes the old custom of hanging up stockings by the chimney and listening for the arrival of St. Nicholas, who rode in a flying carriage and entered the house through the chimney. In 1822, Clement C. Moore wrote a poem for his children entitled "A Visit from St. Nicholas," better known as "'Twas the Night Before Christmas." This poem soon appeared in many magazines, and children throughout the country fell in love with the generous, merry figure who would reward them for good behavior by giving gifts on Christmas Eve. In Clement C. Moore's poem, St. Nicholas takes on an American identity all his own. The cheery, upbeat message of St. Nick's visit is directed at children, and this helps develop the new tradition of celebrating Christmas at home with family.

In America, the time-honored old Saint Nicholas is transformed from a stately bishop into a tiny, winking elf, clad in fur, and sporting a pipe. This friendly image took firm hold in drawings by famed American illustrator Thomas Nast. Of the illustrator's many drawings of Santa Claus, the most famous was published in 1881. Thomas Nast dreamed up Santa's outfit of a wide belt and red tunic and his home at the North Pole. Through the years, Nast's cartoons changed Santa from a small elf to a full-size man, gave him a longer beard and bigger belly, and added more warmth and twinkle to his personality.

Based on the Nast tradition, the colorful, rosy-cheeked look of Santa that is popular today descended from a series of Coca-Cola advertisements created in the 1930s. Artist Haddon Sundblom introduced the first full-color Coca-Cola Santa ad in 1931. Sundblom's model was a retired salesman whose plump and cheery face made the American Santa Claus even more friendly and inviting. The artist's Norman Rockwell-like style brought new warmth and coziness to Santa's image. These qualities have evolved into today's familiar interpretations of Santa as a jolly grandfather figure with a chubby waistline, bright red cheeks, and laughing face that warms the hearts of children of all ages.

Old World Traditions get a New American Twist

Like Santa Claus, the Christmas tree has old European roots and has become more Americanized over time. Evergreen trees were used in German medieval mystery plays to represent the Tree of Paradise from the Adam and Eve story. At the end of such plays, the tree also symbolized eternal life promised by Jesus Christ. Even though the mystery plays faded into history, the evergreen tree stayed on as a homey symbol of the winter season. German families brought a small tree into the home at Christmas time as a symbol of the Christ child, and decorated the boughs with cutout paper flowers, bright foil, apples, sweets, and other fancy treats. The tradition spread throughout Europe and came to America with the German immigrants. Originally, the Christmas tree was small, no more than three feet high, and placed on a small table. But in the American cities, the fashion changed as Christmas became more of a spectacle in the home. The new tree of choice was king size, with the top brushing the ceiling of a beautifully decorated parlor room. Small gifts that had traditionally hung on strings from the branches were now piled up around the base of the tree.

Another feature of Christmas that took a uniquely American turn in the nineteenth century is the tradition of Christmas lights. Candles were traditionally placed on the Christmas tree to symbolize Jesus as the light of the world. In spite of a series of clever clips and gadgets designed to hold the candles in place, candle flames often set fire to Christmas trees. The solution to this problem came with Thomas Edison's first patent of the light bulb in 1879. In 1882, Edward Johnson of New York City claimed to be the first person to put electric lights on his Christmas tree. More than one hundred years later, Christmas lights on outdoor trees and houses are some of America's most elaborate and exciting rituals of the season.

FOLLOWING PAGE:

The Christmas Crèche at the LaSalette Shrine in Attleboro, Massachusetts, portrays the night of Jesus's birth. The first nativity scene was created by St. Francis of Assisi in Greccio, Italy, in the thirteenth century, in which he used townspeople and animals to create a live Bethlehem scene.

RIGHT: *Standing alone
in the wilderness,
this tree, that would
be welcome in any
shopping mall in the
lower forty-eight states,
adds a holiday glow
to a cabin near Fair-
banks, Alaska. It will
survive for many more
Christmases to come.*

OPPOSITE: *Waiting for
Santa on Christmas
Eve, a young boy looks
and listens for signs of
the reindeer and sleigh
in the sky. The visit
from Santa described
in Clement C. Moore's
poem "Twas the Night
Before Christmas"
from 1822 was the in-
spiration of this enduring
American tradition.*

One of the practices that helped shape the unique American Christmas in the last half of the nineteenth century was gift-giving. Protestants regarded wealth and success as God's reward for living a good, virtuous life. Sharing gifts with the family at Christmas became an important way of celebrating this ideal. Gifts strengthened the bonds between parents and children and became a socially acceptable way for single men and women to show affection for each other. From the start, toys were the most commercially successful Christmas gifts, because children were the focus of the holiday. Other very popular gifts included religious items such as beautifully packaged bibles, prayer books, and Christmas annuals. Printing was inexpensive, and books were a highly prized gift item. Books with religious themes remained popular holiday gifts for generations. One American publishing house, Augsburg, took up the early American tradition again in the 1940s with the publication of Christmas treasuries filled with artwork, religious verses, and stories, and continued to publish them every year until 1997.

Gift-giving has its roots in two ancient Roman holidays, Saturnalia and Kalends, which both fell in December. During Saturnalia, gifts were given to the poor, and on the New Year's celebration of Kalends delicacies and gifts were given as tokens of good wishes for the upcoming year. In eighteenth– and nineteenth-century America, gift-giving was popular during New Year's celebrations. Not until the transformation of Christmas into a domestic holiday in the last half of the nineteenth century did it become a traditional part of that holiday as well.

As the nation expanded from the Atlantic seaboard westward, and finally from the plains to the West Coast, immigrants brought new cultures and new flavor to the American Christmas. It is a season that continues to evolve, with children now sending letters to Santa via e-mail and retired couples opting to take luxurious Christmas cruises. What unifies the holiday for Americans everywhere runs deeper than beloved images of Santa, candlelight church services, or favorite network re-runs of It's A Wonderful Life and Rudolph the Red-Nosed Reindeer. What ties it all together is the American spirit of ingenuity, and the ability to comfortably mix both the sacred and social aspects of the holiday. This book celebrates the many ways in which this remarkable blend takes shape throughout the land. Each photograph is a unique glimpse into Christmas in America, from the suburbs to the countryside to the cities.

CHAPTER ONE

SUBURBAN AMERICA—
AN IDEAL CHRISTMAS

Calmer than the city and more convenient than the country, the suburb offers the American dream of a house, a yard, and a neighborhood community. From the long chain of suburbs surrounding Los Angeles to the small communities outside St. Louis, suburbs of all kinds share a few common elements. Driving—to work, to the schools, and to the shops—is a big part of suburban life. And putting all the shops in one convenient spot, usually away from a downtown center, has created an entire mall culture. Christmas in the suburbs revolves around the individual home, the neighborhood school, the community church, and, perhaps most actively, the local mall.

The suburbs around America's big cities have been growing steadily since the end of World War II. From the new estates fringing the desert outside Phoenix to the luxury developments of western Connecticut, suburbs represent an entirely modern type of community. Suburban traditions are very young, and they center on an interesting mix of preferences about the good life. Having a single family home with plenty of lawn that separates people from each other is isolating, but neighbors find a way to create their own small social community. The most intimate hours of Christmas—the family dinner and opening gifts on Christmas morning by the tree—are celebrated in the home, but Christmas in the suburbs is also a community holiday. Everyone in America shops for Christmas presents. And almost everyone in the suburbs shops at the mall.

LEFT: *A personal visit with Santa gives every child the chance to ask for the Christmas gift of his or her dreams. The first real-life department store Santa appeared in J. Lichtenstein & Sons in New York City in 1888.*

"A Shrine to Shopping"

Christmas shopping officially begins on the day after Thanksgiving. The season is ushered in with the first appearance of Santa Claus at the end of the Macy's Thanksgiving Day Parade. Gift-giving is big business, of course, and American shoppers spend more than 100 billion dollars in stores during the holiday season. Another one billion is spent on Christmas trees. It's impossible to ignore the ads and the hype and the commercial mania of Christmas, but gift-giving is such an important part of the holiday that the shopping spree must go on.

Retailers have long tried to make buying gifts as central to the Christmas holiday as giving and receiving them. The first store to feature a real-live Santa Claus was J. Lichtenstein & Sons of New York in 1888. Other stores soon followed, and John Wanamaker's in Philadelphia even set up a special direct-to-Santa telephone line in the toy department. An uncle or father may dress up as Santa at home, but St. Nick has a way of making many appearances at the mall before Christmas eve. One of the highlights of the modern family Christmas is to measure

OPPOSITE: *New England is the birthplace of the Christmas caroling tradition in America, with the first caroling group organized in Boston in 1908. Here, carolers gather on the Town Common in Thompson Hill, Connecticut.*

RIGHT: *With over $100 billion spent in stores during the holiday season, the shopping mall has become one of the major attractions of the modern American Christmas. A wonderland of Christmas trees highlighs the dazzling decorations in the Hilltop Shopping Mall in Richmond, California.*

RIGHT: *A toy soldier stands guard over a dazzling light display in Pleasantville, New Jersey. Annual Christmas presentations of Tchaikovsky's ballet,* **The Nutcracker,** *have made the toy soldier a popular image of the season.*

a child's growth year after year through annual pictures taken with Santa Claus at the mall or the local department store.

In today's suburbs, the shopping mall overflows with special holiday events, including live music, caroling, holiday cooking demonstrations, elaborate mechanical Christmas displays, and Christmas movies at the multiplex theater. The biggest mall in the country, Minnesota's Mall of America, is a shrine to shopping with 454 stores and 26 million square feet of shopping space. At Christmas, shoppers are treated to live musical shows and hundreds of special holiday events. Tourists from all over the world come to this northern shopping mecca during the Christmas season to have the distinction of buying gifts at one of the most famous malls in the world.

Since the mid-1980s, many shoppers flock to the suburban malls in search of the holiday season's must-have toy. This gold-rush sensation started with the Cabbage Patch Kids doll, and every year since, toy manufacturer's have tried to create the same excitement over one special toy that will be the hit of the season. In 1997 it was the Tickle Me Elmo, and in 1998 it was the furry little Furby. The more difficult the toy is to find, the more valuable it is to parents who want to create the ideal Christmas for their children.

LEFT: **Charming, beautifully decorated storefronts make Christmas shopping a special outing for the entire family. Suburban residents often make a trip into the big city to take advantage of one-of-a kind specialty stores that offer unique gifts not found in the local mall.**

Christmas Lights: Suburban Splendor

Creating the perfect Christmas in the suburbs also includes decorating the house, inside and out, as well as buildings and parks. Lights and lawn decorations have become hallmarks of certain neighborhoods, drawing carloads of visitors and creating a new Christmas tradition—taking a night-time drive to see the lights.

America owes its fascination with Christmas lights to the Irish, who brought the tradition to New England in the nineteenth century. The custom of burning candles on Christmas Eve began in Ireland in the sixteenth century, when King Henry VIII declared the Anglican Church the official church of Ireland and closed all the Irish monasteries. Priests went into hiding in the countryside, and Irish Catholics were no longer allowed to attend Mass. On Christmas Eve night, Irish families lit candles and placed them in windows to signal to a priest who may be in the area. The door was kept unlocked in the hope that the priest would make his way to the house and bless the family by saying Mass in their home.

In the nights of December, America glows with suburban neighborhoods that have brought Christmas lighting to an art form. Each state has its own famous areas where the tradition has developed over the years, from house to house and block to block. In Marble Falls, Texas, a small town west of Austin, the lakeside park is ablaze with more than a million electric lights during the holidays. This marvelous sight, as well as many other amazing displays in central Texas, draws visitors from throughout the state. Dozens of blocks in Jacksonville, Florida, vie for attention with yards filled with mechanical dolls,

BELOW: Suburban America glows and sparkles with personality at Christmas time. A favorite tradition is taking an evening drive through town to view each neighborhood's original decorations on houses, rooftops, and lawns.

LEFT: *An old New England scene shines through the night as part of Springfield, Massachusetts' annual Bright Nights display.*

running train sets, Santas flying through the air, nativity scenes, illuminated snowmen, giant musical bows on garage doors, lighted fountains, and Mickey Mouse figures that celebrate the Disney World atmosphere of Florida. In one subdivision, a real Santa Claus strolls the grounds, turning the neighborhood into a virtual Christmas theme park. In the small Denver suburb of Littleton, Colorado, Main Street is the focus of a charming light display that brings everyone downtown to stroll through open shops and listen to carolers. In the larger Denver suburb of Aurora, fans of Christmas lights take motorcoach tours that wind through dozens of neighborhoods shining with a breathtaking variety of displays.

In the Dyker Heights section of Brooklyn, New York, homeowners outdo themselves with displays that have become a national attraction. In this small Italian neighborhood, which to Manhattanites is a suburb of New York City, herds of electric reindeer frolic next to life-size nativity scenes and millions of lights create canopies over the street. One lawn contains a complete reproduction *of A Christmas Carol*, with larger-than-life characters from the Charles Dickens story moving about and flying through the air. Seven-foot Santas greet visitors on doorsteps, brass bands play in the streets, and people in Christmas costumes parade from block to block giving away candy. Cars with license plates from Texas and California drive by, sharing the road with busloads of tourists. Once a year, this small, quiet neighborhood becomes an over-the-top Christmas show. As one resident told *The New York Times*, "It's a Brooklyn thing."

In Newport Beach, California, Christmas lights take to the water with hundreds of decorated boats cruising the harbor. The colored lights illuminate the night and cast beautiful reflections in the water. Up along the north coast of California in Eureka, an unusual parade of lights takes a twinkling course through the streets. A Christmas convoy of big semi-trailer rigs decorated with thousands of lights slowly moves along the crowd-filled route. Christmas is for truckers, too.

RIGHT: *Nearly one million lights illuminate this home near Red Lion, Delaware. Many neighborhoods from coast to coast have earned special status as tourist stops for their elaborate lighting displays, and attract visitors from every corner of America each year.*

RIGHT: *Typical of the seasonal spirit found all across America, this scene, "The Singing Christmas Tree," from an annual pageant presented by the Sheridan's Hills Baptist Church in Hollywood, Florida, features a full choir accompanied by a symphony orchestra. Originally a presentation for church members only, it is now offered to the community-at-large.*

LEFT: Hot-air balloons of light form the highest layer of this amazing display near Bear, Delaware. Light displays such as this, with non-religious images, illustrate how the American Christmas is a rich blend of both sacred and popular culture.

LEFT: The original meaning of Christmas—sometimes forgotten in the frenzy of holiday preparations—is remembered in this light display, part of the Festival of Christmas Lights in Ocean City, Maryland.

Sacred Scenes

Drive-ins may be a thing of the past in the suburbs, but outside Tulsa, Oklahoma, a truly original drive-in attracts holiday visitors every year. The Drive-Through Living Nativity includes live animals and a cast of sixty people. In the privacy of their own cars, visitors glide through while listening to a cassette tape that describes the nativity story—and gives directions on where to turn for the

next scene. This American-sized Christmas display is open every night of the season and is a uniquely American twist on the tradition of the outdoor nativity scene.

Christmas decorations inside the home often include a small nativity scene placed beneath the tree, on the fireplace, a table, or even on top of the television set. The very first nativity was created by St. Francis of Assisi in 1223. On the feast day

ABOVE: White-gloved, stylish young performers present a holiday dance routine at the Cashera Performing Arts Center in Williamsport, Pennsylvania. Celebrating the season with school and community arts productions puts Christmas dazzle in towns of all sizes.

OPPOSITE: Three earnest young tap dancers patiently await their next cue in a rehearsal for the big Christmas show in Williamsport, Pennsylvania. Children's' pageants and choral concerts brighten the hearts of all ages in every town across the country at Christmas time.

FOLLOWING PAGE: *Like a beacon in the snow, a quaint bed and breakfast glitters with Christmas cheer in Bayfield, Wisconsin. What holiday traveler could resist such a warm welcome?*

LEFT: A school band in Madison, Connecticut dons Santa hats for the annual Christmas parade. In towns throughout the country, Christmas parades draw crowds and bring the community together to either participate or watch the pageant of bands and floats.

RIGHT: Santa drives a garland-decked wagonload of participants in the annual Wassail Parade in Woodstock, Vermont.

OPPOSITE: Santa and Mrs. Claus on parade in a bright red sleigh in Connecticut. The jolly, portly, and very merry American Santa Claus descends from the fourth-century bishop, St. Nicholas, whose feast day has been celebrated on December 6 in Europe for hundreds of years.

ABOVE: Dressing up like Mary, Joseph, and other figures from the Christmas story is part of American Christmas pageantry. In this procession, children in Rangeley, Maine, sing carols as they stroll through the crowd.

of the Nativity that year, he organized the setup of a live Bethlehem scene in the town of Greccio, Italy, which included animals, townspeople, an ox, and an ass. The nativity scene or Christmas crèche became a popular custom throughout Europe, and in many areas it was traditional to build an enormous display made of hundreds of figures.

The sacred aspects of Christmas in suburban

areas are also expressed in candlelight Christmas Eve church services. The evening or midnight Christmas Eve Mass began in medieval Europe, where it was commonly believed that Jesus was born at midnight. In America's Catholic and Protestant churches, the late evening or midnight service often includes a living nativity scene as well as individual candles for each person to hold while favorite Christmas

hymns are sung. During the holiday season, Sunday school children take to the stage in pageants, dressed up as characters from the Christmas story. In modern churches throughout the suburbs of Chicago, Dallas, Boston, Nashville, Miami, Los Angeles, Seattle, and throughout the country, children perform in Christmas plays that echo the miracle plays of old Europe.

The Christmas pageant takes on Biblical proportions at the Crystal Cathedral in Garden Grove, California, a suburb of Los Angeles. This giant, all-glass church presents visitors from around the world with an annual "Glory of Christmas" production featuring hundreds of performers, live animals, flying angels, dazzling lighting, and special effects, and the booming sound of the cathedral pipe organ. On

ABOVE: Every year, people from all over the Los Angeles area flock to the Crystal Cathedral in Garden Grove, California for sumptuous Christmas productions and candlelight services.

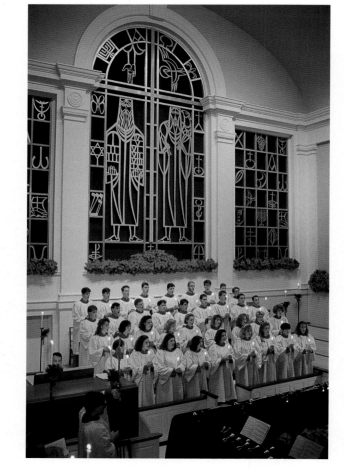

RIGHT: *Music is a special part of the season, with favorite hymns and carols sung in both sacred and public spaces. Many traditional hymns and carols, such as "O Little Town of Bethlehem" and "It Came Upon A Midnight Clear" were written by New England ministers in the nineteenth century.*

Christmas Eve, thousands of people from Los Angeles and its entire suburban community attend the cathedral's seven candlelight services, including the midnight service which is given in both English and Spanish.

In addition to church services and children's plays, school concerts bring neighborhoods together to enjoy the music of the season. Choral concerts, band and orchestra programs, and student ballet productions of *The Nutcracker* fill the schools and community centers. A handful of colleges have earned a special distinction for their holiday concerts, some of which are televised on network television. St. Olaf College of southern Minnesota, for example, draws a huge crowd for its annual Christmas Festival, and the television broadcast has become a beloved holiday tradition throughout the country. In the West, people from outlying communities drive to Salt Lake City to hear the annual Christmas concert given by the Mormon Tabernacle Choir in the tabernacle on Temple Square. This large-scale event is also televised.

LEFT: *Congregations, such as this one in the chapel of Bucknell University in Lewisburg, Pennsylvania, join in with the choir during an annual Christmas concert to sing familiar carols. In many churches, the lights go out for the final carol, "Silent Night," which is sung in candlelight.*

OPPOSITE: *Handbells ring out Christmas church music with a joyful sound that is heard only at this time of the year. After weeks and sometimes months of practice, handbell players master their entrances with the one or two bells to which they are assigned.*

TVs and Patio Parties

Reminiscing about holidays of the past includes memories of favorite television programs that have taken their place as part of the traditional American Christmas. Adults who grew up watching "Rudolph the Red-Nosed Reindeer," "How the Grinch Stole Christmas," and "A Charlie Brown Christmas" every December watch them again with their own children, year after year.

If watching animated specials on television is a homebody part of Christmas, the tradition of the block party balances out the season with plenty of social flair. Whether it's the entire block or just the people next door, suburban parties celebrate the bonds that exist between close neighbors. In the colder states, the Christmas party is held inside one family's home, and in warm states the party is set up outdoors on the lawn or the patio beneath canopies of lights and other decorations. Neighborhood parties bring a casual, relaxed pace to the holidays.

Wandering in and out of the house, neighbors take in the scent of apple cider warming on the stove with sticks of cinnamon, or refill their cup of eggnog—a drink with a long history as an official Christmas beverage. In old Europe, when upper-class householders were obligated to treat their reveling guests at Christmas time, they served

LEFT: Love at first sight. Giving gifts at Christmas is a relatively new tradition in America, begun in the mid 1800s. Though everyone is pleased to be remembered at Christmas, there is no greater pleasure than seeing a child receive an unexpected treat.

LEFT: Gifts are usually opened on Christmas Eve in the evening or early Christmas morning. Exchanging gifts has been a part of winter celebrations for thousands of years, beginning with the ancient Roman festivals of Saturnalia and Kalends which were held in December.

OPPOSITE: At a resort in Wayne County, Pennsylvania, little girls help decorate a new batch of Christmas cookies. Gathering around the kitchen table to decorate cookies is a tradition that brings the family together.

this rich drink made of eggs, sugar, milk, and whiskey. It was important to offer a special, rare drink in exchange for the goodwill that the householder expected from the "lads of misrule" for the rest of the year. Glögg is another festive drink offered at neighborhood Christmas parties, particularly in the Midwest. This spicy concoction from Scandinavia is served warm and contains red wine, sherry, cardamom, cinnamon, cloves, raisins, sugar, and whiskey.

From leisurely night drives through brightly lit streets to long hours at a crowded mall, Christmas in the suburbs blends the most traditional customs with the newest, ever-changing ones. A dream home filled with all the trappings of the season, a 10,000-bulb display on the roof and the lawn, gifts to meet everyone's wish list under the tree, and a dining room filled with family and neighbors on Christmas Day is perhaps the ideal suburban Christmas. But in any neighborhood, the electric joy of the season forms a happy bond for everyone—Christmas shared by the entire community.

RIGHT: *Baking gingerbread houses and other fancy baked goods is a Christmas tradition that dates back to very early times. In ancient Europe, farmers celebrated the gift of the harvest during the winter solstice in December. Christmas cookies and fruitcake also stem from this early custom, which was later adopted by Christianity.*

LEFT: *With Grandfather at the head of the table, a family says grace before eating Christmas dinner. Not even the most crowded airports or highways can dampen the spirits of those who travel far and wide every year to return home for Christmas and a home-cooked meal of turkey, ham, or roast beef.*

OPPOSITE: *A festive table spread with holiday treats, proudly displayed by two veteran bakers. Christmas is a time for each generation of the family to come together over great food and good company.*

CHAPTER TWO

Rural America —
A Country Christmas

Gliding down a snowy country road in a horse-drawn sleigh, singing carols on an evening hayride, listening to the distant bells of the town church, and feasting on Christmas day in a decorated Victorian farmhouse are just some of the delights of an American country Christmas. The centuries-old farms of New England are covered with lights that can be seen for miles. In Eastern Tennessee, wreaths and lights add a warm and welcoming look to homes tucked away in the hills.

Because Christmas is a family holiday, many people gather at the oldest family homesteads, such as the farm. For generations, this custom has helped keep the vision of the Victorian Christmas alive, complete with heaps of garland, holly, pine boughs, wreaths, and other greenery lining the warm wood interior of the house. This country look is copied everywhere, from city apartments to shopping malls, because the Victorian theme is the most enduring concept of Christmas.

BELOW: Not all Christmas celebrations take place in the home. Some families choose to travel and discover new settings for their holiday enjoyment, as has this group taking a sleigh ride at Nestlenook Inn in Jackson, New Hampshire.

OPPOSITE: Many American Christmas decorations are based on prototypes from New England, which were fashioned from natural, seasonally available materials. In addition to the Christmas wreath on the door of this Connecticut house, the top of the doorway sports an "appleboard" plaque, suggesting the abundant hospitality within.

35

RIGHT: *Not far from the North Pole, the tradition-al home of Santa Claus, stands this Inuit igloo, surmounted by lighted whalebone arches. Located near Barrow, Alaska, it is one of the northern-most places where one can experience Christmas in America.*

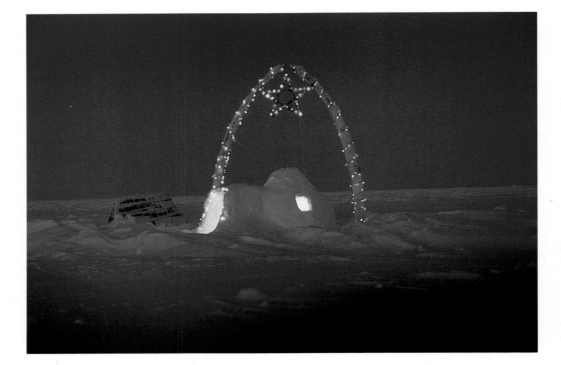

LEFT: *People are often captured by the Christmas spirit; they enjoy it to the fullest, and nothing remains undecorated. However, this lighted birdhouse is not only whimsical but recalls the gentle teachings of St. Francis of Assisi, the creator of the nativity scene which is so much a part of Christmas tradition.*

OPPOSITE: *At the heart of every rural community is the church, and no more so than at Christmas time. Even while everyone is at home and preparing to sleep, the lighted Christ-mas tree proclaims the timeless seasonal message of peace and good will.*

Christmas Dinner and Country Outings

In the country, the kitchen is the heart of the home—especially during the holidays. The idea of Christmas dinner as the greatest feast of the year goes back to pagan traditions, when the bounty of the harvest was celebrated during the winter solstice in December. Women baked special breads and cakes to express reverence for the gift of

bread and to find favor with the gods of the fields. Even after Christianity swept away many ancient pagan customs, the custom of honoring bread in December remained and was blended into the new religion. From these ancient customs come the fruitcakes, pies, and cookies that are such a traditional part of Christmas today. The timeless ritual lives on in American kitchens every year, as children form cutout cookies of Santa, stars, candy canes, and Christmas trees.

The specialties of Christmas dinner varied from country to country in Europe, and each of them are represented in the traditional American Christmas. A dinner of roast beef comes from the English, where cattle herds were thinned out before winter set in and various beef dishes served up in November and December. Christmas ham has long been a favorite in the continental countries. And in every land of the Old World, wild game such as grouse, geese, and even swan, were winter favorites. In America, the fowl that graced the earliest Christmas dinner tables was the wild turkey, and this bird continues to be the most popular centerpiece of Christmas dinner.

One of the enduring desserts of Christmas, mince pie, stems from a custom begun when the Crusaders returned to England. The faithful came back from the Holy Land with a variety of Oriental spices. Mince pie, filled with flavors from the Lord's native land, was the perfect way to celebrate the Feast of the Nativity.

In addition to the family Christmas dinner, the special foods of Christmas play a role in the traditional social calls made throughout the countryside. Carrying a fancy plate of Christmas cookies, country neighbors drop in on each other to visit and take a look at each other's Christmas trees and decorations.

Another popular country outing at Christmas is to the tree farm. There are one million acres of tree farms in America, at least one in every state. Oregon, Michigan, Wisconsin, Pennsylvania, California, and North Carolina are the biggest producers of Christmas trees, and the number-one

favorite is the balsam fir. When people flock to the countryside to select a tree, they usually find a lot more awaiting them. Many of the farms transform into Christmas theme parks in December, with hayrides, visits with Santa, live concerts, craft fairs, petting zoos, and gift shops.

ABOVE: City dwellers must be content with trees supplied by the seasonal vendor down the block. Rural folk, however, have the advantage of scouring the woods to find and-bring home the Christmas tree that is just right for their family's needs.

RIGHT: Children thoroughly enjoy the Christmas season. They look forward to it for months. An added pleasure for them is to be allowed in the preparation for the holiday, especially the all-important task of choosing the perfect tree.

FOLLOWING PAGE: "Man's Best Friend," faithfully awaits the return of the family to begin the holiday festivities that will enliven this snow-covered Western cabin in the Rockies.

LEFT: **Two angels, tapers ready, await their cue to take part in a Christmas pageant. Acting out the Christmas story is a way for children, not only to participate in the day, but to eventually learn the profound meaning of the holiday.**

LEFT: **Dressed as an angel, and supported by a brace of stalwart canine guardians, this child plays a small but important part in the annual Christmas pageant of Rangeley, Maine.**

OPPOSITE: **Christmas is about the family, and no family member, even the loyal watchdog, is exempt from participating. This woman in rural Idaho seems to have found a willing canine convert to the joy of Christmas.**

43

Home on the Range for Christmas

In the open country of the West, where horse and cattle ranches are separated by hundreds of acres, ranch homes and fences are strewn with lights. Keeping to an old frontier tradition, the West celebrates the season with its own brand of get together: the ranch dance. A tradition since the first "Texas Saturday Night" events with live fiddle bands, the ranch dance brings country people together for weddings, birthdays, and holidays. With the new popularity of country dancing, "ranch-style" dance halls have sprung up everywhere, especially east of the Mississippi. In the large halls, a modern country band either adds to or replaces the traditional fiddle players, but the spirit of the music loses nothing in the translation. Country dances are even a hit in the big cities; in New York City it's common to see executives in three-piece suits stomping to a line dance at a country dance club on a Saturday night. During the holidays, country dance clubs offer special Christmas buffets with western-style barbecue and pumpkin pie.

ABOVE: Special concerts by famous choirs and acclaimed symphony orchestras are an accepted part of Christmas in the big cities. In the countryside, however, people make their own music, singing along—in tune and out—with friends and neighbors at holiday church services.

LEFT: This Michigan farm offers a haven of warmth and good cheer on a cold winter's night. The precise outlining of the buildings in lights suggests a pride in the family homestead that reaches back over many generations.

LEFT: The big day, long waited by children every-where, is finally here for these two Illinois farmboys, running through the snow to have their picture taken.

Las Posadas:
Christmas in the Southwest

Christmas in the west and southwest also reflects the Spanish-Mexican influence on the American frontier. In Kingsville, Texas, the annual Christmas celebration includes street dances, cowboy-style breakfast on the King Ranch, and, as the highlight event, La Posada de Kingsville. Re-enacted throughout the southwest, Las Posadas is a mystery play from Spain that re-enacts Mary and Joseph's search for an inn before the birth of Jesus. Members of the family take on the roles of the Holy Family, and parade from room to room or house to house requesting *posada*, a place to rest. One of the most famous Las Posadas processions in the United States is presented in San Antonio, Texas. Performed at night, this candlelight pageant is led by Spanish choirs, mariachis, priests, and children who parade along the city's beautiful Riverwalk.

In the rural Southwest, Las Posadas is celebrated in the home, with children leading the procession. Pretending to be Mary and Joseph, they go from door to door asking to be let in, but are refused. But when the procession reaches the special room that contains the Christ child's manger, everyone is invited inside, and at midnight the baby Jesus is placed in the manger. After the pageant part of Las Posadas, the party begins, with a colorful piñata filled with treats for the children and a festive holiday feast for the adults.

The enchanting, song-filled Las Posadas pageant has found its way into other regions of the nation, too, even as far north as Seattle.

One of the most beautiful visual images of Las Posadas in towns such as San Antonio, Santa Fe, and San Diego, is the stream of light formed by glowing luminarias and farolitas. Luminarias are small bonfires, usually set ablaze in churchyards before the Midnight Mass. Farolitas are candles placed in small paper bags, weighted with sand or gravel. Throughout southern California, New Mexico, Nevada, Arizona, and Texas, farolitas are lined up in rows along driveways, rooftops, and sidewalks as the lighting of choice for the holidays. The origins of luminarias and farolitas are thought to come from Spain, where small bonfires lit the way to Christmas Eve Mass.

LEFT: *Tradition has it that Santa has many helpers. The large man in the sombrero is one of them. Designated within the Hispanic community of San Antonio, Texas as Santa's cousin, Pancho Claus brings promises of delightful Christmas mornings to the many children who visit him.*

LEFT: *A minor wonder of the holiday season is the way in which so many people find new and individual ways of expressing their love for this special time of year. Here, just outside a home in Dana Point, California, is a perfect example: the native cactus transformed into a riot of humorous, cartoon-like characters.*

OPPOSITE: *The bleached skull, a New Mexico icon, made famous by the paintings of Georgia O'Keeffe, is a common decorative motif in the Southwest. Here it takes on a festive, seasonal flair with the addition of a garland of greenery and a crown of Christmas lights.*

Another import from the Hispanic culture that has become a staple of the American Christmas is the poinsettia, the bright red plant known as the "flower of the holy night" in Central America and Mexico. In America, the flower got its name from Dr. Joel Poinsett, the first U.S. ambassador to Mexico who brought the plants to America in 1828, where they soon became very popular. The bright red leaves of the poinsettia, which surround a small yellow flower, symbolize the star of Bethlehem. The legend of the plant is a charming Christmas story from Mexico, in which a poor little boy wept outside the doors of a church because he had no gift for the Christ child. From the ground where his tears fell sprang a green plant with huge red leaves. He plucked the star-like plant and brought it into the church as a gift for Jesus.

ABOVE: One of the great traditions of Hispanic culture introduced to America, is the procession, Las Posadas . Meaning "the inns," the parade reenacts the story of Mary and Joseph searching for a room at an inn in crowded Bethlehem, just before the birth of Jesus. San Antonio's annual event, shown here, is one of the best-known in America.

ABOVE: One of the most enchanting elements of festivities in the American Southwest is the display of "farolitas." Simply made of candles, surrounded by a paper shade and weighted to the ground by sand, they act as welcoming beacons to friends and neighbors who gather together to enjoy the holidays.

OPPOSITE: Not every part of America is blessed with tall evergreens whose conical shapes fulfill everyone's idea of the perfect Christmas tree. In such southwestern states as Arizona and New Mexico, the exotic and prickly saguaro becomes an unlikely, but striking, substitute.

Christmas in the River Parishes

If the tiny flames of farolitas conjure up images of Christmas in the Southwest; four-alarm bonfires signal the arrival of "Papa Noel" in the River Parishes of southern Louisiana. At seven o'clock on Christmas Eve, the fire chiefs give the signal for torch-bearers to simultaneously light a string of approximately 100 bonfires stretching along both banks of the Mississippi River. Giant flames and sparks leap into the air and burning sugarcane pops like firecrackers.

Christmas bonfires have been a tradition in the region since the eighteenth century, when French (Cajun) and German immigrants began to settle along the banks of the river. For centuries, Europeans had celebrated the summer and winter solstices with bonfires, a tradition that came from an ancient Celtic custom of worshipping the sun with fire. When the immigrants brought this tradition to the New World, they burned their celebration fires on plantation lawns and along the levees. In the early decades, homes were spread along great distances from each other, and Christmas fires only dotted the river. In recent years, the popularity of Christmas bonfires has grown enormously, drawing thousands of visitors in tour buses, motor homes, cars, and riverboats.

The bonfires are built teepee style, supported by a long central pole that is piled up with logs, willow reeds, and sugar cane. In addition to this simple original design, the bonfires have given way to a true folk art form, with massive constructions in the form of everything from plantation houses to riverboats. On November and December weekends, the levees are filled with people building the bonfires and enjoying family-style, spicy Cajun food. When a child asks why the bonfires are built, they hear the story of Papa Noel, the Cajun Santa Claus, who paddles up the river at Christmas to bring gifts to good Cajun children, the bonfires lighting his way.

BELOW: Christmas at the Acadian Village in Lafayette, Louisiana, brightly lit. The brightness is important to local children, because the Cajun Santa Claus—Papa Noel—must have guiding lights as he paddles through the bayous to deliver his presents to them.

OPPOSITE: Santa in jeans riding the back of an alligator? Not the usual image of St. Nick, but a humorous, back-country, bayou, down-home-sophisticated take on that fictional/real character who spreads joy every Christmas, especially to the folks of Lafayette, Louisiana who created this display for us to enjoy.

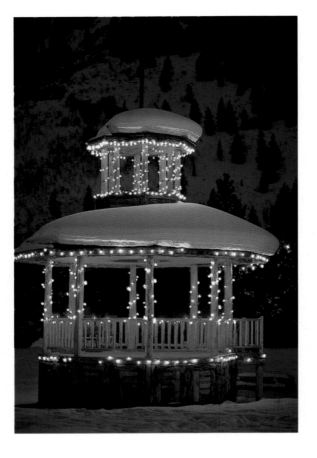

RIGHT: *In summer this bandstand in Aspen Colorado might be the focus of a celebration of the Glorious Fourth. In mid-December, however, though snowbound and deserted, it still gives forth a welcoming glow to commemorate another holiday dear to all Americans.*

Christmas in the Mountains

For skiers and jet-setters, the prime holiday getaway is a luxury resort in the Rocky Mountains, "America's Alps." From the celebrity-studded streets of Aspen, Colorado, to the family-packed tourist attractions of Jackson Hole, Wyoming, Christmas in the Rockies is a high-altitude holiday. The holiday season is about making a fashion statement, about spotting a movie star, and about indulging in rustic luxury at America's finest ski resorts, where the latest designer skiwear is as important as getting a table at the trendiest nightspot.

Looking through the windows of a cozy fireplace lodge, guests behold a spectacular torchlight parade on the slopes on special evenings during the holidays. In the mountains of Idaho, Colorado, and Wyoming, graceful skiers glide down the mountain carrying burning torches that form breathtaking, moving lines of light. In this dazzling display, the ancient rituals of fire are played

LEFT: No section of America, no matter how far removed from urban centers, is immune to the infectious and heart warming spirit of Christmas. This holiday wreath, a European design idea imported to the American Northeast, adorns the fence of a ranch in Sun Valley, Idaho.

OPPOSITE: Aspen, Colorado is one of America's holiday glamour spots, filled with bustling activity, the possibility of spotting Hollywood stars, and such unusual distractions as buggy rides through the snow drawn by a pair of llamas, natives of the Andes who also thrive in the Rockies.

out against the stark white backdrop of mountain snow.

In the East, the Appalachian, Pocono, and Adirondack mountains are filled with woodsy Christmas attractions such as caroling hayrides, light festivals, and outdoor concerts. The beautiful ski resorts in upstate New York, Vermont, and New Hampshire bustle with the flavor of a rustic New England Christmas.

On the more flashy side, the mountains of eastern Tennessee are home to a Christmas theme park courtesy of country superstar Dolly Parton. In November and December, Dollywood becomes a "Smoky Mountain Christmas," with eighty acres of entertainment that include everything from a living nativity pageant to singing Christmas trees. This holiday vacation spot is a fantasyland for children, with steam engine rides, Christmas characters including Mrs. Claus, and teams of sprightly elves, handbell choirs, carolers, and

Santa's Giant Workshop. If visitors are especially lucky, they may get a surprise appearance and concert by Dolly herself.

Christmas in the country and in the mountains, in the bayou and on the plains is celebrated with delightful flashes of regional flair. Each tradition and custom extends a lifeline to earlier Christmases and, in some cases, ancient celebrations of a fire that has never left the human spirit.

BELOW: Dollywood celebrates the timeless traditions of the Christmas season with over two million lights, holiday shows, and much more.

RIGHT: Audiences are enchanted with holiday harmonies and winter wonder at Dollywood's musical production, **Christmas in the Smokies.**

OPPOSITE: The magic of Dollywood, in Pigeon Forge, Tennessee, comes alive with an array of red and white lights, including the magnificent sparkle of the park's Ferris wheel.

FOLLOWING PAGE: In all mountainous resort regions of America, people often like to combine their enthusiasm for skiing and the great outdoors with their holiday celebrations. This inviting scene is typical of many winter vacation spots at Christmas time.

CHAPTER THREE

URBAN AMERICA—
AN ECLECTIC CHRISTMAS

Holidays in the cities are a bustling revolving door of city dwellers flying out, and visitors flocking in. "Home for the holidays" may be the favorite motto of today's Christmas, but the traditional holiday as we know it was actually created in the cities by storytellers, artists, merchants, and manufacturers. This makes Christmas in the city—technically—the most traditional Christmas of all.

In the big cities, Christmas takes on a larger-than-life dimension with stadium-sized theater shows, celebrity tree lighting events, sing-alongs attended by thousands, and store decorations that pull out all the stops. Visiting the live Santa display in a department store and viewing elaborate store window scenes have become as traditional as turkey dinner at Christmas.

Window Dressing, or the Story of the 1000-pound Fruitcake

Along the Nicollet Mall in Minneapolis, Michigan Avenue in Chicago, and Fifth Avenue in New York, visitors line up in front of the biggest department stores to take in the spectacle of modern Christmas window dressing. Music and spoken narratives flow out to the street as the scenes unfold from window to window. Moving mechanical figures enact favorite stories such as *A Christmas Carol,* and *The Velveteen Rabbit,* or new twists on classic tales such as "Alice in Winter Wonderland." Snowy cotton landscapes sparkle with Victorian scenes of animals, puppets, and the Nutcracker.

This entertaining tradition began in the 1800s, when city bakeries competed for holiday business.

In Philadelphia, for example, confectioners came up with the idea of baking huge cakes to display in shop windows for the 1840 Christmas season. Advertised as "mammoth cakes," these super-sized creations became must-see novelties, and shoppers could purchase a piece of one to bring home. One shop featured a cake weighing 250 pounds, and another, 500 pounds. Topping them all was one shop's ad for A "LARGE AND EXTRA MAMMOTH FRUIT CAKE—NEARLY 1000 POUNDS." Another bakery craze in the nineteenth century were window displays made of artfully crafted objects molded of sugar and chocolate. Sausages, loaves of bread, animals, and giant insects—including cockroaches—were carefully sculpted and painted to appear very lifelike.

Other stores quickly caught on to the bakers' clever feats of Christmas advertising, and

ABOVE: Playing out a department store tradition begun over one hundred years ago, Santa listens to a young boy's Christmas want list in the "Ice Gazebo" of the Lenox Square Mall in Atlanta.

OPPOSITE: Visitors from all over the world come to New York's Radio City Music Hall to see the annual Christmas Spectacular, a dance and musical extravaganza, featuring the high-kicking Rockettes.

glorious Christmas window-dressing was soon in full swing on the cities' major shopping streets. The first moving figures appeared in the windows of Macy's New York store in 1898. Since then, themes and styles of the displays have changed every season, sometimes following the current art movement or celebrating pop culture. During the Dada art movement of the 1930s, for example, the Bonwit Teller store in New York called upon Salvador Dali to create a Christmas window. He offered up a bloody-faced mannequin sitting in a bathtub.

In the 1990s, Christmas window dressing is a competitive game because so much rides on the success of holiday sales. In New York City, an extraordinarily unique and over-the-top window guarantees television news cameras and other great publicity. This motivates stores to come up with innovative, one-of-a-kind ideas that will give them an edge over the competition. In this spirit, the Lord & Taylor store stands out from the pack with the world's only hydraulic window displays, and Bloomingdale's, in a recent season, came up with a mysterious method for scenting the sidewalks with the aroma of pumpkin.

ABOVE: *The Christmas season in New York City officially opens at the end of the Macy's Thanksgiving Day Parade, with the appearance of Santa and his reindeer. Watching the parade on television is a holiday ritual everywhere in America.*

OPPOSITE: *A New York police officer, complete with ermine cap and jingle bells, plays Santa for a day to entertain the city's children. Hundreds of charitable events take place at Christmas time, following a long tradition of feeding and clothing the poor during the winter months.*

LEFT: *Every year, Atlanta's Fine Arts Center features a model room, decorated for the Christmas season in a contemporary manner, that evokes both the traditions of the region and the nostalgia all Americans feel during the holiday season.*

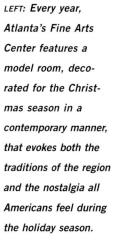

LEFT: *Christmas in downtown Atlanta, Georgia, features vivid arches of holiday lights in Centennial Park. Traditional Christmas events in this Southern city include holiday concerts by the Atlanta Symphony Orchestra and visits with Santa at the Botanical Garden.*

OPPOSITE: *Bright and delicate origami Christmas tree decorations, created by artfully folding paper, are a tradition from Japan which has been adapted by Japanese artisans to enhance the Christmas season in America.*

Christmas for a Song

Carols, hymns, and other traditional songs fill the air of city churchs, streets, and concert halls during the holidays. On the biggest scale, many major cities offer a traditional *Messiah* sing-along, in which hundreds of music-lovers dust off their scores to sing the "Hallelluiah Chorus" and other sections of George Fredrick Handel's beloved masterpiece. This ritual began in New York just after the Civil War, when huge choruses gathered to sing *Messiah* in an armory.

BELOW: A Chicago street musician fights off the winter cold with gloves, a Santa hat, and hot sounds—much to the delight of Christmas shoppers and tourists.

Boston is famous for its costumed, handbell-ringing Christmas carolers and is the birthplace of the American caroling tradition. The first organized Christmas Eve caroling group sang through the streets of Boston's Beacon Hill neighborhood in 1908, and the tradition continues to this day. Many families would hold an open house, opening their doors to carolers and neighbors. Across the river at Harvard, carols are also part of the annual "Christmas Revels" show, a famous celebration of tradition, wit and ceremony. In St. Louis, the Christmas Eve caroling tradition began in 1909, when groups of young people strolled through the streets and stopped to sing in front of homes that had lit candles in their windows.

Some of the most familiar Christmas carols were written by Americans (who also happened to be city dwellers) in the nineteenth century, such as "It Came Upon the Midnight Clear." The words to this classic carol were written in 1850 by by Unitarian minister Edmund H. Sears. A graduate of Harvard Divinity School, Sears is also remembered as one of the first preachers to use the phrase, "Peace on the earth, good will to men." The tune to this carol was composed by Richard S. Willis, an American who became the music director of a church in New York City after studying in Germany with Felix Mendelssohn.

The words to "O Little Town of Bethlehem" were written in 1893 by Phillips Brooks, one of the most highly respected New England clergymen of the nineteenth century. At the age of thirty, Brooks traveled to the Holy Land, and part of his trip included riding on horseback from Jerusalem to Bethlehem just before Christmas. This dramatic trek inspired him to write the verses that every child, to this day, learns by heart. The music was written by Louis H. Redner, the church organist at Holy Trinity Church in Philadelphia where Phillips Brooks was the rector. Brooks gave Redner the words one Saturday, and the organist created this famous setting in time for the next day's Sunday school classes.

Another famous Christmas hymn that American children learn by heart is "Away in a Manger," composed by James R. Murray. The hymn composer

LEFT: *A quartet of carolers on San Francisco's Pier 39 dress in Victorian costumes, a favorite theme of the American Christmas. Victorian style recalls Christmas in old England as well as Charles Dickens' beloved* A Christmas Carol.

could not have dreamed when he published the song in a little book called *Dainty Songs for Little Lads and Lasses in 1887* that his little hymn would become one of America's most beloved Christmas songs. The words were taken from a child's book of poems published by the Evangelical Lutheran Church in North America. For many years it was believed that Martin Luther wrote the poem and the tune, but scholarly research discovered that the piece does not follow Luther's style and is completely unknown in Germany. It was undoubtedly written by an anonymous author in America.

The words and music to the classic Christmas hymn "We Three Kings of Orient Are" were written by New England minister John Henry Hopkins, Jr. This very talented man, when not writing sermons and attending to his church work, was a poet, musicologist, composer, and designer of stained-glass windows.

Non-religious Christmas songs that help create a distinctly American holiday mood include "Jingle Bells," which, oddly enough, doesn't have anything

ABOVE: *Christmas at twilight in Quincy Market: an unusually serene moment in this bustling and popular section of Boston.*

to do with Christmas. This lively song about a snowy sleighride was written by renowned and controversial Unitarian minister John Pierpont, who was ousted from his Boston church in 1845 for his reformist ideas after serving there for more than twenty-five years.

RIGHT: *Holiday decorating in city neighborhoods is an opportunity to express one's personal style. This cheerful Victorian house in San Diego uses a teddy bear beneath a parasol to reflect the sunny character of Southern California.*

Some of the most famous secular Christmas songs come from movies, such as "White Christmas," written by Irving Berlin for the 1942 film *Holiday Inn* starring Bing Crosby and Fred Astaire. Released during the darkest days of World War II, Bing Crosby's recording of "White Christmas" touched the hearts of everyone separated from loved ones by the war, and became an instant hit. The song became such a success that it inspired a movie of its own, *White Christmas*, in 1954, which once again starred Bing Crosby. Another classic Christmas song from the movies is "Silver Bells" from the songwriting team Ray Evans and Jay Livingston. Written for *The Lemon Drop Kid* starring Bob Hope in 1951, the first draft of this song was entitled "Tinkle Bells." When Ray Evans' wife heard the words, she quickly pointed out the more familiar meaning of "tinkle," and persuaded her lyricist husband to change the word. Thanks to Mrs. Evans, perhaps, "Silver Bells" is one of America's favorite Christmas songs and has been recorded by artists of all styles, from Perry Como to the rock group R.E.M.

LEFT: *Shepherd's robes, rustic wood, and fresh hay, in a life-sized nativity scene, are a stark contrast to the modern skyscrapers of Chicago's Daley Plaza.*

OPPOSITE: *Victorian splendor comes to life each Christmas at the Pabst Flemish Renaissance Mansion in Milwaukee, Wisconsin. Built in 1892 by sea captain and beer baron Frederick Pabst, the 37-room home is filled with lavish decorations that celebrate 19th-century style.*

An Urban Christmas Trek

The beginning of any American city Christmas tour must begin in "Christmas City U.S.A.," Bethlehem, Pennsylvania. Founded and named by German Moravians in 1741, Bethlehem is a small town about sixty miles north of Philadelphia. Throughout December, visitors arrive by the busload to view the lights and decorations on the historic homes,

attend candlelight concerts, ride in horse-drawn carriages, and shop for gifts at the *Christkindlmarkt* (Christchild market). Blazing above the town on top of South Mountain is a four-story star of Bethlehem that can be seen for miles.

Another town that vies for attention as a Christmas center is McAdenville, North Carolina, where 400 trees are decorated with hundreds of thousands of red, green, and white bulbs. Some of the trees encircle a lake, which is also the setting of giant light display of Santa and his reindeer. Word has spread about the displays, which began in the early 1950s, and now approximately 300,000 people drive through McAdenville to see the lights at Christmas. As seen in the sign that welcomes you into town, McAdenville dubbs itself "Christmastown."

Heading south we come to New Orleans, where the ancient oaks of City Park twinkle like a fairyland with a million white bulbs. Papa Noel leads a jazz parade down Bourbon Street, and the lacy balconies of the French Quarter glitter with colorful lights. Foot-stomping gospel choirs give concerts at St. Mary's Church, and Midnight Mass at St. Louis Cathedral is the highlight of the holiday for local parishioners. The Reveillon (awaking) dinner, a custom of the early settlers, has recently come back into fashion in the city. After attending midnight Mass on Christmas Eve, the early residents of New Orleans sat down to a large, festive meal to end the fast that began in Advent. Residents and holiday visitors revel in the rebirth of this tradition, feasting on elaborate Reveillon dinners served in December at many of the city's fine restaurants.

Less fancy yet very traditional Christmas feasts served in some New Orleans homes include favorites such as Cajun Deep Fried Turkey, prepared in a big pot outdoors with red pepper, tabasco, and liquid crab boil. Another popular and spicy Christmas dinner enjoyed by Louisiana families is Cajun Baked Ham with side dishes of creamed potatoes, cornbread dressing, and sweet potato pie.

West of Louisiana, beyond the riverside bonfires, the ranch dances of Texas and the luminarias of New Mexico, we come to Christmas in Los Angeles. The city offers spectacular classical concerts, seasonal plays, and, here and there, a peek into the look of Christmas past. The Heritage Square museum, which holds "Lamplight Tours" every December, is a collection of Victorian-era buildings including homes, a church, and a railroad depot. The buildings are decorated in greenery and lights, and history buffs as well as those who love the look of a traditional Christmas tour the grounds.

One of the more unique events of the Los Angeles Christmas is something that could never be duplicated anywhere else—the Hollywood Christmas Parade. This star-studded, band-playing, float-filled extravaganza was launched in 1928 by the Hollywood Chamber of Commerce. The merchants wanted to create a special incentive for people to come to Hollywood Boulevard during the holiday shopping season. The parade has grown into an annual festival that draws more than one million people and is televised throughout the country.

Heading out over the Pacific we come to the American Christmas—island style. In Honolulu and Waikiki, the Christmas season officially begins on a day in early December when the mayor throws the switch to light the giant Christmas tree in front of Honolulu Hale (city hall). Next, he lights up the monkey pod and banyan trees that surround other city buildings and the Iolani Palace. In the stores, reindeer and ornaments frolic in garlands of heavy-scented orchids. Parades in some of the nearby towns feature homemade floats with traditional Polynesian designs, including young women representing Mary dressed in traditional Hawaiian wrap-around dresses.

On Christmas Eve, a candlelight service is given in the historic Kawaiahao Church across from Honolulu Hale. The church was built in 1842, and services are given in the Hawaiian language. Earlier

in the day on Christmas Eve, Santa cruises into Waikiki Beach on a surfboard wearing bright red swimming trunks and carrying a bag of goodies for the children.

Back on mainland, our city trek makes a stop in Seattle, Washington, where parades of brightly lit boats glide through the evening waters of Lake Washington almost every night in December. In addition to the "Christmas Boats," Seattle looks forward to a unique yearly visit from Santa Claus—on water skis. Decked out in a Santa outfit over his wet suit, an anonymous citizen zips over the very cold water every year, waving to his warmly dressed fans on shore.

ABOVE: The Riverwalk in San Antonio, Texas, is the setting for one of America's most famous Las Posadas pageants. The re-enactment of Mary and Joseph's search for an inn at Bethlehem, Las Posadas is a major Christmas tradition in Texas and the Southwest, and gaining ground in other parts of the country as well.

Stretching all the way across the country we come to New York City, where Christmas brightens up every neighborhood, from the Cathedral of St. John the Divine uptown to Times Square to Wall Street. In the first week of December, the enormous Christmas tree at Rockefeller Center is switched on at the high point of a musical program hosted by a different celebrity each year. Nearby, the wildly popular "Radio City Music Hall Christmas Spectacular" taps out holiday cheer with a music and dance review starring the high-kicking Rockettes.

The choral music tradition of New York is as old as the city itself, and every neighborhood is filled with churches that offer special Christmas programs. One of the unique specialties of church music in New York is the presence of many professional singers in the choirs. Paid professionals, they take on extra "gigs" during the holidays and often chase after cabs to get from one service, mass, or concert to the other.

An event that has grown very popular with New Yorkers in recent years is the annual Christmas concert given by Chanticleer in front of the Christmas Tree inside the Metropolitan Museum of Art. This professional male choir is a national treasure that tours the United States and the world. Set around a sprawling, ornate crèche beneath the tree with medieval sculptures scattered

throughout the room, the Chanticleer concerts bring a sublime sound and a moving new tradition to Christmas in New York.

Along Fifth Avenue, the sidewalks are more crowded than any other time of year. Above the intersection at Fifty-seventh street, a huge snowflake makes its annual appearance, suspended above the river of cabs and shoppers. People stand in front of the department store windows to view the amazing displays, wander in and out of stores to shop, take a carriage ride through Central Park, have tea in the

ABOVE: The Radio City Music Hall Rockettes tap their way into Santa's heart every year at the world-famous stage show.

RIGHT: A sculpture of gigantic Christmas tree ornaments dwarfs visitors to the lobby of this New York City office building.

OPPOSITE: The Christmas tree at Lincoln Center, home of the New York Philharmonic, the New York City Ballet, and the Metropolitan Opera is covered with lights and ornaments in the shapes of musical instruments.

FOLLOWING PAGE: Two rows of lacy, white-light angels at Rockefeller Center herald the season with trumpets and draw attention to the spectacular Christmas tree in front of the General Electric Building.

Garden Court at the Plaza Hotel, or walk from Macy's over the Madison Square Garden to take in *A Christmas Carol*.

From church services to Broadway shows, from ice rinks to tea rooms, and from elegant champagne dinners to office parties, Christmas in the Big Apple has an abundance of electrifying good cheer. People are happy in New York during the holidays, and it shows.

In addition to department store Santas and sidewalk Christmas tree vendors, a familiar character in the urban Christmas is the Salvation Army bell ringer. The Salvation Army, a religious and charitable

organization founded in London, held their first dinner for New York City's poor at Madison Square Garden in 1898. To pay for these industrial-sized events, the army hired homeless men to dress as Santa and collect contributions on the street corners. Outfitted with a handbell and a large pot for donations, the Salvation Army Santas became a common sight in New York and other large cities (they no longer wear Santa suits; the bell ringers that do are members of an organization called Volunteers of America). In the 1990s, female Salvation Army bell ringers in New York were outfitted with snappy new suits designed by Donna Karan.

ABOVE: *The famous Tavern on the Green restaurant in New York's Central Park is covered and surrounded by a blazing display of white lights during the holiday season.*

OPPOSITE: *A towering Christmas tree competes with one of the gigantic chandeliers in the lobby of the Plaza Hotel in New York City.*

Confidently guarding the New York Public Library on Fifth Avenue, this is one of a pair of lions which is decorated in a twinkling wreath and giant bow every Christmas season. For formal events, the lions wear shiny black top hats, and when a library room is under construction, they wear large yellow hard-hats.

A sweet deal— the New York Stock Exchange puts on a candy-cane façade during the holidays.

In the medieval room of the Metropolitan Museum of Art, an elaborate 18th-century Neapolitan nativity scene surrounds the base of a tall Christmas tree. A new and growing New York Christmas tradition is the annual concert in front of the tree by the American choral group, Chanticleer.

*"We therefore embrace the present as the most fitting occasion we shall
have of tendering our holiday congratulations to both old friends and new; and . . .
content ourselves by wishing to one and all a cheerful, a merry, and a happy new year."*
—THE *NEW YORK MIRROR* EDITORIAL COLUMN, 1839

Christmas is Forever

The American Christmas is as varied as the nation's
melting pot of cultures. It's a holiday that has bor-
rowed from ancient rituals, Old World traditions,
and trappings of popular culture. Whether held as a
sacred day, a time-honored family celebration, or a
civic holiday, Christmas is ingrained in the hearts
of Americans everywhere.

Although the sentiment of Christmas has endur-
ed throughout the centuries, the style in which
Americans express that sentiment has changed.
Christmas memories that were once recorded in a
colonial family diary are now preserved as full color
movies made with high-tech camcorders. Glowing
candles on the parlor Christmas tree have evolved
into spectacular electric light displays that dazzle
entire neighborhoods. Horse, buggy, and train jour-
neys that brought families together have transformed into airplane trips that sweep people across
the country in a matter of hours.

The spirit of Christmas has not only survived
these changes, but has achieved an even more
American identity along the way. Compared to the
traditions of its European ancestors, America's customs are very new. They will continue to evolve
from decade to decade in the new millennium,
always reflecting the spiritual essence of the people.
From the countryside to the bayous, the malls to the
seaside, the suburbs to the cities, Christmas in
America has always been, and promises to always
be, a celebration of life and love.

*ABOVE: The Old Water Tower, one of Chicago's most
famous landmarks, is drenched in bright lights that
warm the hearts of Christmas shoppers on Michigan
Avenue. This stone building was one of the few
structures to survive the Chicago Fire of 1871.*

*OPPOSITE: Washington, D.C.'s Christmas tree, near the nation's Capitol. Christ-
mas trees inside the White House have been a tradition since the late 1800s.
However, in the early 1900s Theodore Roosevelt banned them, because he
thought cutting down Christmas trees depleted the national forests. Times and
forestry have changed, and today more than 23 trees grace the various rooms of
the White House, including a 12-foot tree for the First Family's private residence.*

INDEX